塑料垃圾

Sharing the Planet | Non-Fiction Series

Copyright © 2022 by Level Learning, INC. and Washington Yu Ying PCS™
Original and Edited Text Copyright © 2022 by Washington Yu Ying PCS™

All rights reserved. No part of this book in whole or part may be reproduced without written permission from the publisher.

Published by Level Learning, INC.

Content Contributors:
Washington Yu Ying PCS™ - Qianyi (Shirley) Zhang, Pearl Zao He You
Level Learning - Jingyao Qi

Illustrations by: Josh Taira

Leveling classification based on Level Learning standard.
For full description, visit www.levellearning.com

ISBN 978-1-64040-059-7
Simplified Chinese Edition

About Level Learning:
Level Learning provides a literacy focused curriculum specifically designed for K-12 Chinese as a Second Language classrooms. Our program offers 20 levels of specific and detailed objectives, leveled texts and passages, mastery-based online assessment, and analytics to enable data-driven instruction. Level Learning reading curriculum for both literature and informational text emphasize grammar and comprehension skills to help teachers develop confident and independent Chinese language readers. The non-fiction series of books are specifically designed to support our informational text course based on multiple national standards. To learn more about our entire offering, visit www.levellearning.com.

About Washington Yu Ying PCS™:
Washington Yu Ying PCS is a Mandarin English dual language immersion International Baccalaureate (IB) World school. Yu Ying's mission is to inspire and prepare young people to create a better world by challenging them to reach their full potential in a nurturing Chinese/English educational environment. Yu Ying's comprehensive IB, dual immersion curriculum equips students with global competencies for success in the real world. As a leader in immersion education, Yu Ying is determined to advance Chinese language programs and global citizenry education by helping other schools create and strengthen their Chinese programs. For more information, email: products@washingtonyuying.org

塑料垃圾是人们丢掉的塑料制品。那些被丢掉的塑料袋、塑料水瓶或塑料玩具等都是塑料垃圾。

塑料制品给人们的生活带来了很多方便，所以很多人都喜欢使用塑料制品。比如说方便的塑料袋，结实的塑料玩具，容易清洗的塑料盒子等等。

但是，这些塑料制品变成垃圾后就成了大问题，因为有的塑料制品成百上千年都不会消失。

另外，塑料也包含一些对人和动物有害的化学物质。

塑料垃圾最后去了哪里呢?有些被回收使用,有些被埋在地下或者烧掉了。也有很多塑料垃圾被留在地上堆积成山,还有的被丢进了海里。

科学家发现,一些被丢进海洋里的塑料垃圾会不停地漂流,最后变成很小很小的塑料颗粒。

这些塑料颗粒会被海洋动物吃掉。人类再吃这些鱼和虾，那些有害的物质就会进入人们的身体。同样，很多陆地上的动物也会吃地上的塑料垃圾，那些有害的物质就会进入动物的身体。

现在，人们知道了塑料垃圾会危害人类和动物的身体健康，会污染环境，所以科学家们发明了新的环保材料代替塑料制品。

其实,每个人都可以通过一些小事来减少使用塑料制品。比如说,用纸袋代替塑料袋;用玻璃盒代替塑料盒;用可以重复使用的水杯代替一次性塑料杯等等。

我们也可以提醒家人或朋友，减少使用塑料制品。从每个人、每件小事做起，我们可以减少很多塑料垃圾。让我们一起保护我们的环境，保护地球生物的健康。

Glossary

	Pinyin	English Definition
塑料	sù liào	plastic
垃圾	lā jī	trash
丢掉	diū diào	to throw away
制品	zhì pǐn	products
袋	dài	bag
水瓶	shuǐ píng	water bottle
方便	fāng biàn	convenient
使用	shǐ yòng	to use
结实	jié shi	durable
容易	róng yì	easy
清洗	qīng xǐ	to wash
盒	hé	box
成百上千	chéng bǎi shàng qiān	hundreds and thousands
消失	xiāo shī	disappear
包含	bāo hán	to contain, to include

	Pinyin	English Definition
有害	yǒu hài	harmful
化学	huà xué	chemical
物质	wù zhì	substance
回收	huí shōu	recycle
埋	mái	to buy
烧	shāo	to burn
堆积	duī jī	to pile up
丢	diū	to throw
科学家	kē xué jiā	scientist
发现	fā xiàn	discover
不停	bù tíng	non-stop
漂流	piāo liú	to float, to drift
变成	biàn chéng	become
颗粒	kē lì	pellets
虾	xiā	shrimp

Glossary

	Pinyin	English Definition
陆地	lù dì	land
危害	wēi hài	to harm, to endanger
污染	wū rǎn	to pollute
环境	huán jìng	environment
环保	huán bǎo	environmental protection
材料	cái liào	material
代替	dài tì	to replace
通过	tōng guò	through
减少	jiǎn shǎo	to reduce
玻璃	bō li	glass
重复	chóng fù	repeat
提醒	tí xǐng	to remind
保护	bǎo hù	to protect
健康	jiàn kāng	health